Life and the Flow of Energy

William B. Rice

Consultant

Leann Iacuone, M.A.T., NBCT, ATC
Riverside Unified School District

Publishing Credits

Rachelle Cracchiolo, M.S.Ed., *Publisher*
Conni Medina, M.A.Ed., *Managing Editor*
Diana Kenney, M.A.Ed., NBCT, *Content Director*
Dona Herweck Rice, *Series Developer*
Robin Erickson, *Multimedia Designer*
Timothy Bradley, *Illustrator*

Image Credits: Cover, pp.1-5, Back cover iStock;
p.7 The LIFE Images Collection/Getty; p.9 (illustration)
Lexa Hoang; p.11 Dreamstime; pp. 9, 11 NASA; p.12
Science Source; pp.14-20,22,25-27, 31 iStock; p.15
(left) Gustoimages/Science Source, (right) Zephyr/
Science Source; all other images from Shutterstock; all
illustrations, Timothy Bradley.

Library of Congress Cataloging-in-Publication Data

Rice, William B. (William Benjamin), 1961- author.
  Life and the flow of energy / William B. Rice.
    pages cm
  Summary: "From microscopic creatures living under
your couch to gigantic elephants roaming Earth, life
needs energy. Energy starts with the sun. Then, it moves
from one animal in an ecosystem to the next animal. This
energy powers all life."-- Provided by publisher.
  Audience: Grades 4 to 6
  Includes index.
  ISBN 978-1-4807-4715-9 (pbk.)
 1. Nutrient cycles--Juvenile literature. 2. Biogeochemical
cycles--Juvenile literature. 3. Food chains (Ecology)-
-Juvenile literature. 4. Biotic communities--Juvenile
literature. I. Title.
  QH344.R53 2016
  577.14--dc23
                                          2015002531

Teacher Created Materials

5301 Oceanus Drive
Huntington Beach, CA 92649-1030
http://www.tcmpub.com

ISBN 978-1-4807-4715-9

Table of Contents

Teeming with Life

No matter where you are in the world, there is always something interesting to see. Life—things that grow, live, and die—is everywhere. *Everywhere*!

When we look across our planet, we see a beautiful and diverse place teeming with life. The living things on the planet are known as **organisms**. They are in abundance in every corner of the globe. There are countless kinds of organisms—perhaps millions of different kinds! Some organisms are microscopic, such as single-celled amoebas (uh-MEE-buhs) or the bacteria that grow and thrive in plenty. They can only be seen with a special lens. Some organisms are enormous, such as the thundering elephants that stomp through Africa and Asia or the elegant whales that swim through the oceans of the world.

Thousands of new species are discovered every year!

Organisms move all over Earth and in every way imaginable. Insects fly and crawl through air, water, and land. Animals climb and fly both high and low. They walk and run at all speeds, from lightning quick to barely seen. They dig and swim with agility and ease. There are more animals in the world than we know, and they can do things that awe and astound us.

One Tough Bunny

The Arctic hare lives in the frozen tundra of North America. It has a thick white coat that keeps it warm in freezing temperatures and allows it to blend into its surroundings. Most animals couldn't survive one winter night in this harsh environment.

kelp

cactus

Plants are also organisms. They live everywhere across the planet, too. We see them growing in oceans, on mountains, in deserts, and especially in jungles. They are often green but also come in all colors of the rainbow. Like every organism, plants have a life cycle.

Organisms grow and multiply. They **breed** offspring that keep the species going. Organisms eat or take in **nutrients**. Organisms may get hurt or sick. But they also recuperate and heal. Some organisms live only a short time, maybe a few days or a few weeks. Some may live for hundreds or thousands of years. But, at some point, all come to the same end. All organisms die.

Compared to a rock or a pile of sand, organisms are quite active. How do they do this? They use **energy**. Energy is the **force** that makes things happen. Energy flows and is stored, changed, converted, and transformed. Organisms use energy to do everything that they do.

But how do organisms get energy? Where does this energy come from? People have been asking these kinds of questions for centuries, maybe even for thousands of years. To answer these questions, scientists study Earth and its **ecosystems**. They also study the organisms and other things that make up ecosystems.

pine

fern

Living Longer

With all the advancements in technology and medicine, people are living longer than ever. Jeanne Louise Calment lived to be 122 years old. When she was 100 years of age she was still riding a bicycle!

Energy and the Sun

The sun is a giant mass of **matter**. Matter is the basic stuff that everything is made of. This book, a plant, you, me—we are all matter. Matter is made of tiny particles called **atoms**. And atoms are made of even tinier particles called *electrons*, *protons*, and *neutrons*. Each type of atom has a different number of particles. Different numbers make different kinds of atoms. Each kind of atom behaves differently from the others. It has different properties, too. All of this makes each kind of atom unique.

An **element** is a chemical substance made of a single type of atom. The sun is mainly made of two elements. They are hydrogen and helium. The sun has lots of matter—lots and lots of matter. Because the sun has so much matter, it also has a lot of **gravity**. Gravity is one of the basic forces of the universe. It helps hold matter together. Gravity puts pressure on matter. Because of this pressure, the sun undergoes a process called **fusion**. Fusion releases many different types of energy—a lot of energy.

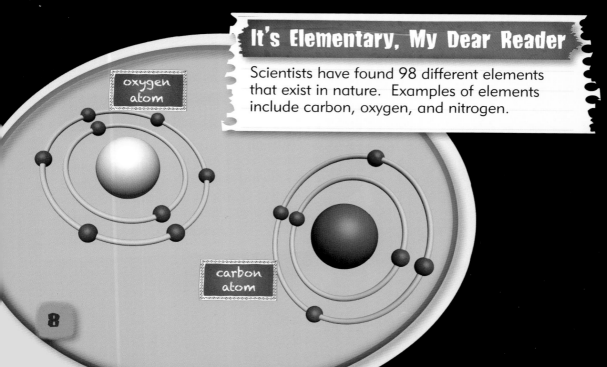

It's Elementary, My Dear Reader

Scientists have found 98 different elements that exist in nature. Examples of elements include carbon, oxygen, and nitrogen.

oxygen atom

carbon atom

8

Fusing Elements

During fusion, elements such as helium and hydrogen fuse, or join, together. Temperature and pressure must be extremely high for elements to combine. Once fusion takes place, energy is released.

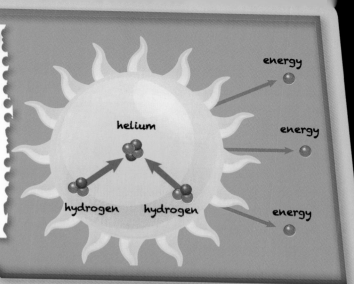

energy

energy

helium

energy

hydrogen   hydrogen

About 75 percent of the sun is hydrogen, about 23.3 percent is helium, and about 1.7 percent is made of elements such as carbon, oxygen, and iron.

Hydrogen atoms in the sun are converted into helium atoms and energy.

Some of the sun's energy is the kind of light that we can see without any special lenses. This is called the **visible spectrum**. The sun also releases energy we can't see, such as X-rays, infrared light, and ultraviolet light. This energy **radiates** away from the sun in all directions. To radiate is to release or spread away from a central point. The sun is the central point.

Some of this energy from the sun hits Earth. The energy heats Earth's atmosphere, the land, and the oceans. Some of this energy radiates to plants. Plants use this energy in a way that makes a difference for all living things. Plants have a special chemical compound called **chlorophyll**. Chlorophyll helps plants change and store energy. Plants use this energy to grow. They shoot roots firmly into the ground. They grow sturdy stems and leaves and produce colorful flowers. And they grow and release seeds into nature.

A World of Color

Light contains all the colors in the visible spectrum. When light hits objects, some of the colors are absorbed and some are reflected. Our eyes only see the reflected colors. For example, a red sweater looks red because it absorbs all the colors in the visible spectrum except for red.

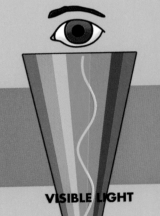

RADIO   **MICROWAVE**   **INFRARED**   **VISIBLE LIGHT**

LONGER WAVELENGTH

LOWER ENERGY

SOHO

BBSO

Studying the Sun

Scientists use special telescopes to study the sun. Some telescopes are on Earth, such as the Big Bear Solar Observatory (BBSO) in California. Other telescopes are on satellites in space, such as the Solar and Heliospheric Observatory (SOHO).

We see the entire visible spectrum of light in rainbows.

ULTRAVIOLET   X-RAY   GAMMA

SHORTER WAVELENGTH

HIGHER ENERGY

Plants and Photosynthesis

So, energy flows from the sun to Earth. On Earth, plants absorb energy. Plants convert and use most of the energy they receive and store the rest. But how do plants convert energy? And what do they convert it into?

Plants convert the sun's energy into chemical energy. They use a process called **photosynthesis**. The chlorophyll mentioned earlier is key. It catches the sun's energy and converts it into other chemicals. The energy causes the chemicals to change their shape. This process is similar to winding up a spring. When the time comes and the plant needs energy, it triggers the chemical, which changes its shape and releases energy like an unwinding spring.

Photosynthesis also produces something every human needs. It produces oxygen as a waste product. Of course, oxygen is not a waste product to us. We can't live without it! We breathe oxygen and then breathe out carbon dioxide as a waste product. Guess what uses the carbon dioxide to live. Plants!

A New Discovery

In the 18th century, Joseph Priestly and Jan Ingenhousz discovered photosynthesis. They performed an experiment in which a mouse was isolated in a sealed jar. Without oxygen, the mouse would die. A plant was also placed in the jar with the mouse. Somehow, the mouse survived. After careful investigation, they learned that the plant produced the oxygen the mouse needed to live.

Little Bundles of Sunlight

Many plants start as seeds. How do seeds start to grow when they have no leaves to capture energy from the sun? Seeds store energy. When seeds are still attached to a plant, the plant stores some of the converted energy in the seeds. Seeds then drop from the plant to the ground, and with the right conditions, they begin to grow.

The glucose produced is used by the plant.

Leaves absorb the sun's energy.

The plant absorbs carbon dioxide.

The plant releases oxygen in the air.

Even prickly cacti use photosynthesis. The sharp spines covering a cactus act as leaves.

Animals and the Sun

I bet you know where we are going next. Maybe you are thinking animals or insects or just creatures in general. If so, you're right. Many animals, insects, and other organisms eat plants. When they eat plants, they not only take in nutrients and minerals, but they also take in that converted energy from the sun. Some organisms eat other organisms. When they do, they get the energy stored in the animal's body. Again, this is energy that started as sunlight and then radiated through space, into Earth's atmosphere, into plants, and then to other organisms.

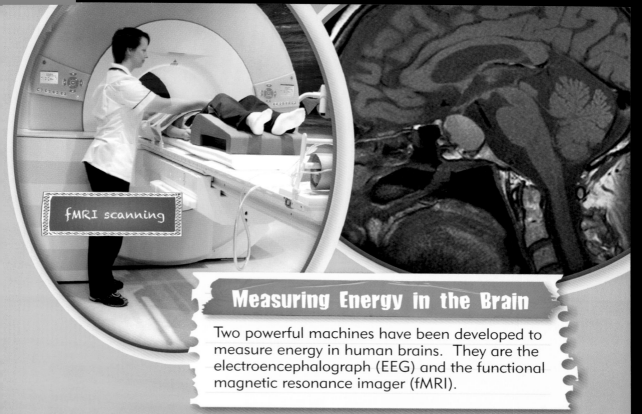

fMRI scanning

Measuring Energy in the Brain

Two powerful machines have been developed to measure energy in human brains. They are the electroencephalograph (EEG) and the functional magnetic resonance imager (fMRI).

All these different organisms use energy from the sun. How do they use it? Just look around and watch these creatures in action. They fly and climb and run and jump. Most creatures rest, but even then they are using energy to help pump blood through their bodies, breathe, and stay warm.

You can even watch yourself. You use energy for many things. Energy helps you breathe. It helps your heart pump blood throughout your body. It helps you digest the food you eat. In fact, you are using energy as you read these words. Your brain is using energy to see the words and understand them.

Your brain uses more energy (about 20 percent overall) than any other part of your body, even though it makes up only 2 percent of your weight.

Cold- and Warm-Blooded

Though most animals get energy from plants or other animals, some animals need energy directly from the sun. Animals such as lizards, snakes, and certain bugs need to bask in the sun to stay warm. *Basking* means "to lie out in the open and take in energy from the sun." Animals that get energy this way are called *cold-blooded.* The scientific term is *ectothermic.*

Most animals, including humans, do not need direct energy from the sun to stay warm. We get our warmth by using food energy. We are warm-blooded, or endothermic. But even though we are warm-blooded, we still depend on the climate and the sun to keep things warm. When it's cold, we put on more clothes to help. And when all is said and done, it still feels good to go out in the sun on a cold day and feel the warm rays.

warm-
blooded

You're Getting Warmer

It's simple to figure out which animals are warm-blooded and which are cold-blooded. Mammals and birds are warm-blooded creatures. So, if there is fur or feathers covering its body, it is most likely warm-blooded.

cold-
blooded

One reason that butterflies sit and rest on plants is to absorb warmth and energy so they can fly more.

Happy Medium

Warm-blooded animals need to stay warm *and* cool! To cool off on a hot day, warm-blooded animals sweat and pant. Staying out of the sun and moving to a shady area is another way these animals stay cool. And although they have fur or feathers keeping them warm, during the summer they shed their extra fur to keep them at a comfortable temperature.

The Energy of Waste

All organisms release waste materials. Waste is a **byproduct**. It is made as the result of nutrient **consumption**. Waste is produced when the body gets all it can use from its nutrients, or food. But even though these remaining materials are called "waste," they are still useful. There is some energy left in them! There are some organisms that can use these materials as their energy and nutrient sources. These organisms are called **decomposers**. To decompose is to take things apart and break them down. Decomposers turn plant and animal parts back into basic chemicals and elements. Plants use these chemicals and elements to grow, process, and function. Without decomposers, there would be no new plant life. With no new plant life, there would be no new animal life. Each form of life is dependent on the others.

This process of consumption and waste is all part of the energy cycle. And the sun's flowing energy makes it all happen!

Maggots

Maggots are fly larvae. They are sometimes used to remove dead tissue from people. They eat only dead tissue but leave living tissue alone.

Earthworms are decomposers that eat dead plants.

Decomposers are nature's sanitation workers. They break down and use dead matter so new life can grow.

Dig In!

Nature's big decomposers include insects, bacteria, mold, and fungi.

mold

Energy Exchange in Ecosystems

Looking at life on Earth, we can see the sun's energy flowing. Every plant and animal participates in the energy flow. Without this flow, there would be no life. In a way, life is energy flowing and transforming.

We see this energy flow in different ecosystems. It is easy to see how the sun's energy flows and supports all life there. In forests, trees and ferns fill the landscape. Birds, deer, mushrooms, and bugs share in the exchange of energy that begins with the sun and plants. In deserts, cactuses and yucca plants grow. Lizards and tortoises eat the plants, and animals such as coyotes may eat them. In grasslands, grasses wave while trees and shrubs dot the land. Big herds of grazing animals such as bison roam. These herds are supported by the sun's energy, which is captured in the vast stretches of grasses there.

herd of bison

Checks and Balances

Even the tiniest insect plays an important part in the flow of energy. Think about a cricket. It is food for many animals, such as lizards, birds, and even humans! But it also breaks down dead plants and recycles nutrients in soil. It can even pollinate flowers!

Ecosystem is short for "ecological system."

Herbivores

Herbivores are animals that eat only plants. Large herbivores need to eat a lot of plants to get their energy. Elephants need to eat plants for up to 18 hours each day to get all the nutrients and energy they need!

Energy exchange is a simple idea. It all comes down to interdependence. All living things in an ecosystem depend on one another. They need one another to survive. It begins as the sun radiates its energy to plants. Plants use this energy to produce their nutrients. Animals consume the plants. They take in the energy stored there. Other animals eat those animals. Then, they absorb the energy. Plants and animals die. Decomposers get their energy from dead matter. Decomposed materials nourish the soil. It helps new plants grow.

The sun continues to send out energy. This is a cycle of energy and renewal. And it happens because every living thing must be nourished through nutrients or food. What a simple but brilliant system! Energy is just a salad away!

Energy Flow

The sun's energy flows to producers (plants). Herbivores are primary consumers because they are the first to get plant energy. Small carnivores are secondary consumers because they get energy next, although some of it is lost. Large carnivores are tertiary consumers, and they get the least amount of the sun's energy.

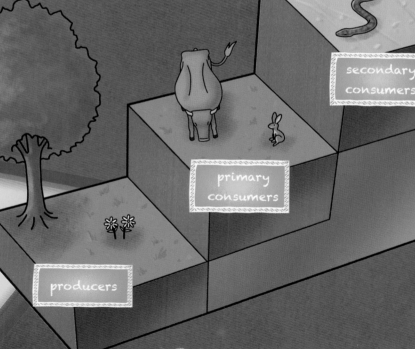

tertiary consumers

secondary consumers

primary consumers

producers

Only about 0.01 percent of the sun's energy reaches tertiary consumers.

Energy in the Ocean

Because plants capture the sun's energy, they are, in a way, the basis for life on land. But what about oceans? They cover more than 70 percent of Earth's surface, and they're filled with all kinds of life. We don't see big majestic oak trees or gigantic redwood trees in our oceans. We don't see beautiful rosebushes or fields of wheat or corn there, either. So, how does the sun's energy support life in our oceans? Are there plants in our oceans that are the basis for life? The answer is yes. But, as with everything that lives in water, the plants there are rather unusual to our eyes. These plants are especially adapted to living in very salty water all the time. Some plants are actually microscopic organisms called *phytoplankton*. Kelp and seagrass are bigger kinds of sea plants that we can see with our eyes. They collect energy from the sun just as land plants do. They use photosynthesis to convert and store energy for use in the same ways.

Other Flows of the Sun's Energy

Energy from the sun warms ocean water. Water particles absorb the sun's energy and evaporate into the atmosphere. This makes clouds that eventually drop water back to Earth in the form of rain and snow. Sometimes, the atmosphere holds so much water energy that big storms form and become hurricanes, typhoons, and tsunamis.

kelp

phytoplankton

seagrass

Thousands of species live in the ocean's kelp forests.

Sun-sational!

Think about this. Every time you eat a sandwich, an apple, or a piece of cake, you are eating a little piece of sunshine—in a way! The sun is the source of all energy on Earth, and that energy is infused through all life on our planet. Energy may be passed from plant to animal to decomposer, but it's the sun's energy all the same. It's in carrots, beans, hamburgers, and popcorn. It's in geese and ducks and goldfish. It's in you and me.

Life could not be life without energy. All living things need ongoing influxes of energy to stay alive. We cannot create that energy from nothing. All energy on Earth, no matter what, starts with the sun.

When we need more energy, we eat nutritious food. But that food isn't the energy source. The sun is. So, sit right down and help yourself to a big bowl of crispy, crunchy sunshine! You'll feel energized in no time.

Won't Live Forever

The sun is old. It's very old. But it won't live forever. Eventually, the sun will run out of enough hydrogen to continue the fusion process. The sun will die, in a way, and so will all life on Earth. But that's billions of years from now.

Scientists estimate that only about 0.1 percent of the sun's energy is needed to power all of the people, plants, and animals on Earth.

Think Like a Scientist

Can you capture the sun's energy? Experiment and find out!

What to Get

- aluminum foil
- black paper
- box-cutter knife (adult use only)
- food to cook
- newspaper
- plastic wrap

- plate
- ruler
- tape
- thin cardboard box (a pizza box works great)

What to Do

1 Ask an adult to cut a flap in a pizza box. Cut along three sides and fold the flap back so it stands up when the box is closed.

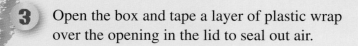

2 Tightly wrap foil around the inside of the flap. Tape the foil to the back of the flap.

3 Open the box and tape a layer of plastic wrap over the opening in the lid to seal out air.

4 Place food on the plate, and place it on black paper. Close the box lid, but keep the flap open and directed at the sun during peak sun hours (11:00 AM to 3:00 PM). Prop the flap open with the ruler.

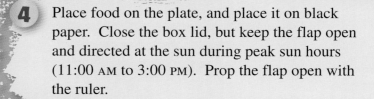

5 Your "solar oven" heats to about 93.3°C (200°F). Adjust your cooking time according to this temperature. Stir food as needed. Be careful not to burn yourself!

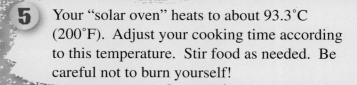

Glossary

atoms—the smallest particles of a substance that can exist by themselves

breed—to produce offspring

byproduct—something that is produced during the production or destruction of something else

chlorophyll—the green substance in plants that makes it possible for them to make glucose from carbon dioxide and water

consumption—the act of eating or drinking something

decomposers—organisms that break down and feed on dead plants and animals

ecosystems—communities of living and nonliving things in particular environments

element—a basic substance that is made of atoms of only one kind and that cannot be separated by ordinary chemical means into simpler substances

energy—power that can be used to do something

force—a push, a pull, or a turn on an object

fusion—a process in which the nuclei of atoms are joined

gravity—a force that acts between objects, pulling one toward the other

interdependence—related in such a way that each needs or depends on the other

matter—anything that has mass and takes up space

nutrients—substances that living things need to grow

organisms—living things

photosynthesis—the process in which plants use sunlight to combine water and carbon dioxide to make their own food (glucose)

radiates—sends out energy in the form of rays or waves

species—a group of plants or animals that are similar and can produce young

visible spectrum—all the light waves in the range humans can see

Index

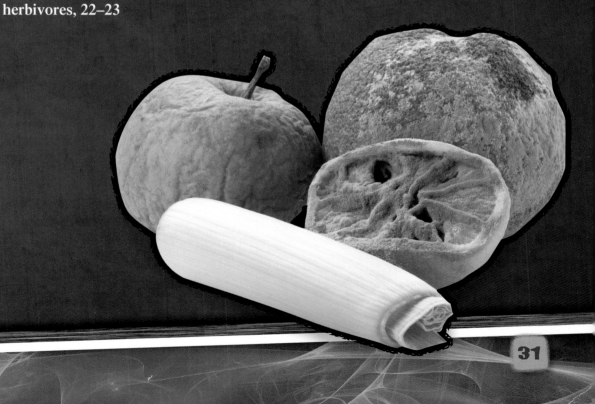

Energy Signs

Find an outdoor location where you can be comfortable for about 30 minutes. You might sit on a big rock, climb a sturdy tree, or sit on a park bench. As you sit, look carefully all around you. Notice the signs of energy that are everywhere. Challenge yourself to list as many as you can during the half hour. Challenge a friend to do the same. Who can get the most? (Even writing your list is a use of energy!)